D0897376

Torah and Trails

A Photographic Trail Guide Connecting Judaism with Nature

Photography and Text by Margery Diamond

Torah and Trails

MOUNTAIN ARBOR PRESS

MOUNTAIN ARBOR
PRESS
Alpharetta, GA

Photography and Text Copyright © 2018 by Margery Diamond
Website: http://www.margerydiamondphotography.com

All rights reserved. No part of this book may be reproduced or
transmitted in any form or by any means, electronic or mechanical,
including photocopying, recording, or any information storage and
retrieval system, without permission in writing from the author.

ISBN: 978-1-63183-349-6

Printed in the United States of America   0 4 2 4 1 8

♾ This paper meets the requirements of ANSI/NISO Z39.48-1992
(Permanence of Paper)

Photo: Heart Tree, Raven Cliffs Wilderness, GA 2014
Cover Photo: Pounding Mill Overlook, Blue Ridge Parkway, NC 2014

TABLE OF CONTENTS

Photo: Garden in Nelson, New Zealand 2017

MEDITATION

Psalm 92

"It is good to give thanks unto God,
And to sing praises unto Your name, O Most High:
For You, O God, hast made me Rejoice in Your work;
I will glory in the works of Your hands."

טוֹב לְהֹדוֹת יְיָ: וּלְזַמֵּר לְשִׁמְךָ עֶלְיוֹן.
כִּי שִׂמַּחְתַּנִי יְהֹוָה בְּפָעֳלֶךָ, בְּמַעֲשֵׂי יָדֶיךָ אֲרַנֵּן.

Tov l'hodot l'Adonai ul'zameir l'shimcha elyon. Ki simachtani
Adonai b'fo-olecha b'maasei yadecha aranein.

Photo: City Park, Atlanta, GA 2013
VIII

INTRODUCTION

In the Bible, God tells Abraham to *"For all the land that you see I will give it to you and your seed to eternity..."* *Genesis (13:15)*

In creating this guide, I drew on my experience of walking down trails in a multitude of places. *Torah and Trails* can go everywhere you go. It is appropriate for all age groups from 10 to 120. You may take a simple walk or spend time training and preparing for a wilderness mountain hike. Make time to see, discover and wonder.

Carry this guide with you and allow your heart and mind to explore all that comes your way. No matter where your journey leads, I trust that *Torah and Trails* will continually inspire you to explore the many connections between Judaism and Nature.

Photo: Chinquapin Wilderness Trail, Glenville, NC 2014

FOREWORD

People say that spirituality was born outdoors. And to a certain extent they are correct.

We build incredible cathedrals and sanctuaries meant to inspire the words of sacred text and those structures are awe-inspiring. But our humanity is far too often lived indoors; the cold existence of interaction with others takes place in climate-controlled spaces with soft texture and remarkable décor. We become conditioned to what has been artfully concocted for our benefit.

But spirituality, the aha moments that take our breath away, these are moments for which we cannot prepare and moments which are beyond fabrication. In the text before you, Margery Diamond returns the Torah, the sacred text of the Jewish people and the foundational story of the Bible and the Quran, to the realm of its birth. You will encounter gorgeous photos captured by Margery's own lens and learning meant to illumine the accompanying scriptural text. The three merge together in this volume – the visuals capture the eyes, the learning captures the head, and the text captures the heart – to present a new perspective.

Happy Trails...and Happy Torah,

Bradley G. Levenberg, Rabbi
Temple Sinai, Atlanta, GA

Photo: South Island, New Zealand 2017

WATER
מים
MAYIM

Photo: Heading South, Tybee Island, GA 2014

1

LISTEN and UNDERSTAND / SH'MA

"Hear, O Israel, Adonai is our God. Adonai is One!"

שְׁמַע יִשְׂרָאֵל יְיָ אֱלֹהֵינוּ יְהוָה אֶחָד!

Sh'ma Yisrael Adonai Eloheinu, Adonai Echad!

The *Sh'ma*, a prayer that we say often, proclaims God's unity. To hear means to listen, and this prayer instructs us to hear and understand.

You are invited to discuss with your trail mate what is wondrous about the place you find yourself. Speak about something that catches your eye. Listen to what your companion tells you. Listen carefully enough to repeat what you have heard them say.

Actually, everything is "WOW!"

Photo: White Owl Falls, Nantahala National Forest, NC 2017

3

POINT ON A TRAIL / SHEHECHEYANU

"Praise to you, Adonai our God, Sovereign of the universe, for giving us life, sustaining us, and enabling us to reach this season."

בָּרוּךְ אַתָּה יְיָ אֱלֹהֵינוּ מֶלֶךְ הָעוֹלָם, שֶׁהֶחֱיָנוּ וְקִיְּמָנוּ וְהִגִּיעָנוּ לַזְּמָן הַזֶּה.

Baruch atah Adonai, Eloheinu Melech haolam, shehecheyanu, v'kiy'manu, v'higianu laz'man hazeh.

A few times a year the Lake Glenville dam is opened, and water goes from three separate streams into one gigantic roaring waterfall. It is beyond amazing to witness.

Choose a place on your trail that is notable in some way. Stop and admire. Take time to truly see all that makes this spot memorable. Look, listen and smell in order to enjoy with all your senses.

If anyone is there for the first time, you can recite the *Shehecheyanu* blessing. This prayer brings an awareness of the awe and specialness of the experience and acknowledges God's hand in the world of nature.

Photo: High Falls, Glenville, NC 2014

HAVDALAH BLESSING / PRAYER

"Praise to you, Adonai our God, Sovereign of the universe, who separates between the holy and the profane."

בָּרוּךְ אַתָּה יְיָ, אֱלֹהֵינוּ מֶלֶךְ הָעוֹלָם, הַמַּבְדִיל בֵּין קֹדֶשׁ לְחוֹל.

Baruch atah Adonai, Elohaynu Melech ha'olam, hamavdil bayn kodesh lechol.

Havdalah is the ceremony that comes at the end of Shabbat, the seventh day, and separates it from the rest of the week. The prayer calls to mind the differences between light and dark; between Israel and the other nations; between good and evil. The braided *havdalah* candle represents the opposing forces of good and evil existing side by side. It reminds us to stop and pay attention to meaning and purpose.

Waterfalls can be beautiful and at the same time treacherous. The dramatic force of the water is dangerous and sometimes frightening. The pools that form at the base are deep and cold. Yet at the same time, their music soothes my soul and carries away my worries. It is a space in which I find myself most at peace.

Photo: Falls on Dodd Creek, Raven Cliffs Wilderness, GA 2017

WATER / MAYIM GENESIS (1:9)

"Waters flowed to their gathering places and dry land appeared."

וַיֹּאמֶר אֱלֹהִים יִקָּווּ הַמַּיִם מִתַּחַת הַשָּׁמַיִם אֶל־מָקוֹם אֶחָד וְתֵרָאֶה הַיַּבָּשָׁה וַיְהִי־כֵן.

Va'yomeir Elohim yikavu hamayim mitachat hashamayim el makom echad v'tay-rapheh hayabasha vayhi-chayn.

The Israelites wandered in the desert for 40 years, and yet the Jewish people did not perish. God provided fresh water as it was needed. In *Midrash*, we learn that it is because of the merits of Miriam that the source of water followed the Israelites through the desert. Water gave life to the Jewish people and continues to be an integral part of many life cycle events.

Water is a critical resource for a community. Lake Glenville is a beautiful lake where I have often paddled. It is a spiritual experience to boat, swim, play and pray in this space.

Photo: Lake Glenville, NC 2015

BLESSING FOR HAND WASHING / PRAYER

"Praise to you, Adonai our God, Sovereign of the universe, Who has sanctified us with Thy commandments and bidden us wash our hands."

בָּרוּךְ אַתָּה יְיָ אֱלֹהֵינוּ מֶלֶךְ הָעוֹלָם אֲשֶׁר קִדְּשָׁנוּ בְּמִצְוֹתָיו וְצִוָּנוּ עַל נְטִילַת יָדַיִם.

Baruch atah Adonai, Eloheinu Melech haolam, asher kid'shanu b'mitzvotav v'tzivanu al n'tilat yadayim.

We perform the ritual of washing hands before eating bread or matzah. Washing a corpse before burial (*Taharah*) is a Jewish responsibility. We wash after escorting the departed to their final resting place. *Mikvah*, a ritual of purification and transformation, remains a meaningful experience for many Jews today. Water must be protected as an essential ingredient of nature.

I visited this magnificent coast line with a friend early this year. Walking alone, I am filled with memories of the many other beaches I have loved. It is at the shore that I feel God's hand in creation. It is a visible reminder of life everlasting.

Photo: Guanacaste, Liberia, Costa Rica 2018

SEA OF TALMUD / YAM ha'TALMUD

"Praise to you, Adonai our God, Sovereign of the universe, who calls us to holiness through mitzvot, commanding us to engage in the study of Torah."

בָּרוּךְ אַתָּה יְיָ אֱלֹהֵינוּ מֶלֶךְ-הָעוֹלָם אֲשֶׁר קִדְּשָׁנוּ בְּמִצְוֹתָיו וְצִוָּנוּ לַעֲסֹק בְּדִבְרֵי-תוֹרָה.

Baruch atah Adonai, Eloheinu Melech haolam, asher kid'shanu b'mitzvotav v'tzivanu la'asok b'divrei Torah.

Go and visit the seashore often and throughout the year. It never fails that when I go, there is something I've never seen before.

Torah study is just that way. Each time you read a passage or say a prayer, you may see it in a different light or from a different perspective and have a unique, personal response.

Both the beach and Torah are alive with information that one can spend a lifetime learning. Each time you walk the shoreline or chant a prayer, you may come away with a greater respect for all that you choose to study and explore.

Photo: Cabretta Beach, Sapelo Island, GA 2014

TREES AND FOREST
עץ ויער
EITZ V'YAIR

Photo: Graveyard Fields, Blue Ridge Parkway, NC 2011

16

SEASONS / ECCLESIASTES (3:1)

"To everything there is a season and a time to every purpose under the heaven."

לַכֹּל זְמָן וְעֵת לְכָל-חֵפֶץ תַּחַת הַשָּׁמָיִם.

Lakol z'man v'et l'chol chayfetz tachat hashamayim.

Fall is the season when nature fills our eyes with brilliant colors – winter white, spring green, and summer blue – each has its own time.

Jewish history is filled with both beautiful and ugly events. Pogroms and World War II were dark and evil times. The establishment of the State of Israel in 1948 was especially joyful.

What do you recognize about your own life events? Honor and cherish the important dates, times and occasions in your life.

Photo: Patterson Gap, Clayton, GA 2014

LOOK CLOSELY / PROVERBS

"Look at what is inside as well as its covering!"

אל תסתכל בקנקן אלא במה שיש בו!

Al tistakel ba-kankan ela be'ma she'yesh bo!

The popular proverb "Don't judge a book by its cover" is based on this Jewish teaching.

Look closely! You may discover a colony of bugs that may have made their home here. A "Days Inn" for insects is a different way of looking at a dead, decaying, rotted tree.

When your life is affected by trauma or tragedy, given time, you may begin to understand that there may also be gifts as a result of these experiences. Judaism teaches us to look beyond the immediate and explore the possibility of a deeper meaning.

Photo: Chinquapin, Glenville, NC 2014

PATHS / PROVERBS (3:17)

"Its ways are ways of pleasantness, and all its paths are peace."

דְּרָכֶיהָ דַרְכֵי-נֹעַם; וְכָל-נְתִיבוֹתֶיהָ שָׁלוֹם.

D'rachehah darchei no-am v'chol n'tivoteha shalom.

Trail markers are there to guide you along your way. Guidance is important if one is to learn and experience nature safely. Maps and markers point the way to explore and discover new paths.

Torah has an order, and we follow it in each of the weekly *Shabbat* services as well as in Torah study. The *Seder* (order) is discussed and interpreted at the Passover table by Jews throughout the world.

Following the markers gives us a better understanding of the subject, whether it is nature or Judaism.

Photo: Sam Knob Trail, Pisgah National Forest, NC 2014

BOUNDARIES / LEVITICUS (25:23)

"The land shall not be sold for eternity for the land is Mine and you are but strangers journeying with Me."

וְהָאָרֶץ לֹא תִמָּכֵר לִצְמִתֻת כִּי־לִי הָאָרֶץ כִּי־גֵרִים וְתוֹשָׁבִים אַתֶּם עִמָּדִי.

V'ha-aretz lo teemacheir l'tz'metoot ki li ha-aretz ki gayrim v'toshavim atem imadi.

God created the world, and we have the opportunity to treat it responsibly with loving care and respect.

In Judaism, we strive to stay on the path of righteousness within the bounds of Jewish law. Sometimes our path leads us to a sign that indicates "*NO trespassing.*" Here, as in life, we have many choices.

Learning how to show respect for the laws of both nature and Torah helps to make us more responsible human beings.

Photo: Chinquapin, Glenville, NC 2015

RIGHTEOUSNESS / TZ'DAKAH Deuteronomy (15:7-8)

"If there is a needy person among you...do not harden your heart...
Rather, you must open your hand and lend whatever is sufficient
to meet the need."

כִּי־יִהְיֶה בְךָ אֶבְיוֹן מֵאַחַד אַחֶיךָ... לֹא תְאַמֵּץ אֶת־לְבָבְךָ
וְלֹא תִקְפֹּץ אֶת־יָדְךָ מֵאָחִיךָ הָאֶבְיוֹן: כִּי־פָתֹחַ תִּפְתַּח אֶת־
יָדְךָ לוֹ

Ki y'hiyeh v'cha ev-yon may-ahchad ache-cha... lo t'ahmaytz et
l'vav'cha v'lo teekpotz et yadcha ma-ahchecha ha-evyon. Ki fato-
ach teeftach et yadcha lo.

Being mindful of the needs of others is a way of practicing social
responsibility. Every traveler should leave a place better than it was
when they arrived. Act righteously and "Leave No Trace."

Leaving a pile of ready-to-burn firewood at a campsite is only one
example of a way to show kindness to a future camper. Adding leaves to
a shelter floor keeps the ground soft and dry for the next occupant.

Photo: Wood Pile, Chinquapin, Glenville, NC 2014

ANCESTORS / TALMUD

"As my ancestors planted a tree for me, so I plant for future generations." Ta'anis (23a)

כי היכי דשתלי לי אבהתי שתלי נמי לבראי

Ki hayche d'shtalti avhati shatalti nami liv're'i.

In services, we say the names of our Jewish ancestors, Abraham, Isaac, Jacob, Sarah, Rebecca, Leah and Rachel. We think about their courage, faith and loyalty to God.

We are reminded of parents in the faces of their children. Something a child does or says brings to life memories of the ancestor whom they resemble. In that way, they live on forever in our hearts.

Look carefully at the bark or burl of a tree trunk. You may see a face there. Pay attention to its message and learn from the experience.

Photo: Mariposa Grove, Yosemite National Park, CA 2011

MOUNTAINS
הרים
HARIM

Photo: Jungfrau, Switzerland 2009

SPIRITUALITY / PSALM (121)

A Song of Ascents "I will lift up my eyes unto the mountains: from where shall my help come?"

שִׁיר לַמַּעֲלוֹת: אֶשָּׂא עֵינַי אֶל־הֶהָרִים מֵאַיִן יָבֹא עֶזְרִי.

Shir la'ma'alot. Esa aynai el he-harim me'ayin yavo ezri.

Water pours from the mountain tops in Milford Sound whenever it rains. I feel fortunate to have witnessed this happening on a trip to New Zealand. These mountains are a visible reminder of the power of prayer and nature.

Psalm 121 is carved into the rafters of the Solomon Chapel at Blue Star Camps. It is here that I first felt the power of prayer. Mountains invite me to pray, and I find solace whenever I am in their midst.

Photo: Milford Sound, Fiordland National Park, New Zealand 2017

GARDENS / TALMUD

"It is forbidden to live in a town that has no garden or greenery."
Talmud Yerushalimi, Kiddushin (4:12)

אָסוּר לָדוֹר בְּעִיר שֶׁאֵין בָּה גְּנוּנִיתָא שֶׁל יֶרֶק.

Asur lador b'ir sh'ayn bah ginunita shel yerek.

Look for medicinal or edible plants and flowers in the midst of the mountainside's wild growth. Dwarf iris bloom wild in the early spring and may be used as a spice or medicinally. Rare turks cap lily makes a beautiful addition to a garden salad.

Sunflower seeds and berries are a source of vitamins. Blackberries, blueberries, mulberries and grapes grow wild in the mountains.

Mushrooms are a mountain delicacy. There are many that look almost the same, and a mistake can be deadly. Positively identify everything you intend to taste.

Judaism encourages us to consider all food miraculous.

Photo: Greenwich, CT 2017
33

34

TRAIL HIGH POINT / GENESIS (1:31)

"And God saw everything that God had made, and behold, it was very good."

וַיַּרְא אֱלֹהִים אֶת־כָּל־אֲשֶׁר עָשָׂה וְהִנֵּה־טוֹב מְאֹד.

Va'yar Elohim et kol asher asah v'hinei tov m'od.

At a trail's highest point, you can sometimes see a 360 degree view. It takes strong legs and stamina to reach a spot with this kind of elevation. It is definitely worth the effort. When I have a view as expansive as this one, it confirms my belief in a higher power. A mountain top awakens my sense of wonder.

Look for the lessons in nature and in Judaism that speak to you. It is important to be aware of all that is around you. Be open to discovery as Judaism is multifaceted. Take time to look inside yourself and see how you fit into the whole picture.

Photo: Double Knob, Glenville, NC 2014

EARTH IS FOREVER / ECCLESIASTES (1:4)

*"One generation goes and another generation comes,
but the earth abides forever."*

דּוֹר הֹלֵךְ וְדוֹר בָּא וְהָאָרֶץ לְעוֹלָם עֹמָדֶת.

Dor holech v'dor ba v'ha-aretz l'olam omedet.

This iconic image has been part of the Yosemite scenery for millions of years. It is a challenging climb and only experienced climbers can safely manage it. The hiking trail is extreme and requires a permit. Yet for generations, outdoor enthusiasts consider it a must-do in their lifetime.

Our predecessors, with their lessons of life and the wisdom of experience, enrich and support our future. It makes sense to research the past in order to prepare for what may come our way. We may learn from our past as we continue to grow into our future.

Photo: Half Dome, Yosemite National Park, CA 2011

DESTINATION / PSALMS (104:24)

"How great are Your works, God, You make them all with wisdom. The world is full of your creations!"

מָה־רַבּוּ מַעֲשֶׂיךָ יְיָ כֻּלָּם בְּחָכְמָה עָשִׂיתָ מָלְאָה הָאָרֶץ קִנְיָנֶךָ.

Ma rabu ma'asecha Adonai, kulam b'choch-mah a'see'ta, ma'l'ah ha'aretz kin'ya-necha.

No matter where or how far away your path may take you, it is always nice to be safely home. Psalms 104:24 is a prayer that may be recited upon a safe return.

Its words of praise for the creation of the world and all its creatures speak to the very essence of this book. You may find that because of your experiences in nature you have developed a better understanding not just of the world, but of yourself.

Photo: Valley View, Yosemite National Park, CA 2011

LIFE FORCE / GENESIS (2:7)

"Then God formed man of the dust of the ground, and breathed into his nostrils the breath of life; and man became a living soul."

וַיִּיצֶר יְהוָה אֱלֹהִים אֶת־הָאָדָם עָפָר מִן־הָאֲדָמָה.

Va'yee'tzer Adonai Elohim et ha'adam afar min ha'adamah.

Torah teaches that our body returns to the earth and the soul lives on with God. This view of several ridges looks out over the mountains of Tennessee. At this height, I can fill my lungs with clean, crisp mountain air, and feel happy to be alive.

My early years as a camper and counselor at Blue Star Camps at the foot of Mt. Pinnacle in Western North Carolina inspired my appreciation for the powerful presence of a mountain. Today, time spent in the mountains is a visible reminder of the numerous connections of nature to Jewish thought and practice.

Photo: Mountain Ridges, Townsend, TN 2012

ABOUT THE AUTHOR

Margery Diamond spent her childhood summers in the mountains of Western North Carolina at Blue Star Camps. Living Judaism filled her heart with the experience of an outdoor Jewish community. For more than six decades, she has continued to study the earth and its connection to her faith.

A retired educator, her focus is now photography. A visual artist, Margery uses her passion for natural beauty to produce photographic images that capture the rich stillness and timeless scope of nature.

Studying her craft and traveling widely, Margery brings an array of shape, light and color to her viewers. Her prizewinning images are on exhibit throughout the world. She is published in national and regional magazines. Her gorgeous images are available as photographic prints on paper, canvas or metal as well as in book format.

Margery wants her photographs to make a difference.

CONTACT

margerydiamond@gmail.com
http://www.margerydiamondphotography.com/
http://www.facebook.com/margerydiamondphotography

Photo: Looking Glass Falls, Pisgah National Forest, NC 2013

ACKNOWLEDGMENTS

Thank you to Blue Star Camps and the Popkin family for introducing me to the concept of pairing nature with Judaism in 1950. My gratitude to Dr. Gabe Goldman whose belief and trust were there as the idea for *Torah and Trails* began to take form in my mind. My deepest appreciation to Bobby Harris and UAHC Camp Coleman, birthplace of the first edition.

To my Temple Sinai Clergy: Rabbi Ronald M. Segal; Rabbi Bradley G. Levenberg; Rabbi Samantha Shabman; and Cantorial Chair Beth Schafer, thank you for your enthusiastic support and encouragement.

To my photography teachers, John Mariana, David Akoubian, Kevin Adams and Kathryn Kolb, much appreciation for sharing your expertise and friendship. Georgia Nature Photography Association, Women In Focus, Roswell Photographic Society and Southeastern Photographic Society have all contributed to my store of knowledge.

My deepest gratitude to hiking friends – Bonnie Rubin, Carol Mentonelli, Hank Aldort, Wendy Lipshutz, Tom Mukon, Howard Kaplan, and Wendy Alpine – who willingly trekked by my side carrying photography equipment and supporting me on many an outdoor adventure.

This book received the brilliant editorial eye of my friend, Berylann Strada who poured over each and every page diligently and gave me the confidence to complete the project.

To my cousins: Dr. Nisha Zenoff, Dr. Jeanne Shaw (OBM) and Rabbi Joseph Shaw, thank you for being there for me as I follow in your footsteps.

Heartfelt appreciation to my entire family, especially my grandchildren, Brooke, Benjamin and Ashley. Thank you to my son, Bret, whose memory serves as a constant reminder to live life to the fullest. You all have opened my heart and taught me the value of love.

Photo: Whitewater Falls, NC 2015

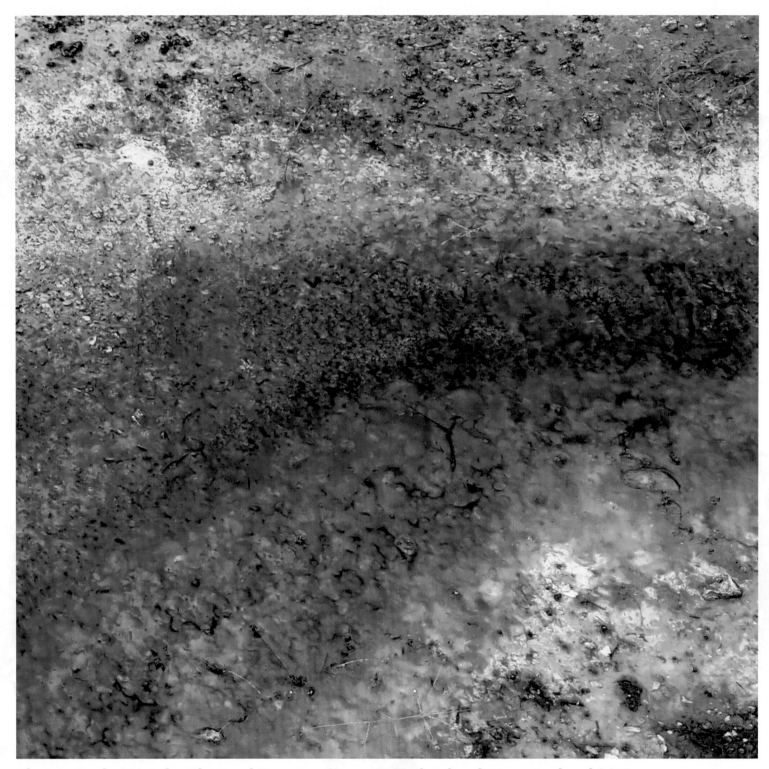

Photo: Orakei Korako Thermal Reserve, Taupo, North Island, New Zealand 2017